THE PENGUIN PO

OXFORD
and Oxfordshire

In Verse

Antonia Fraser was brought up in Oxford where her father, then Frank Pakenham, was a don at Christchurch. The greater part of her education was also had in Oxford – at the Dragon School which she attended for four years and later at Lady Margaret Hall, Oxford, where she read History.

Antonia Fraser is the author of three noted historical biographies: *Mary, Queen of Scots*, which won the James Tait Black Memorial Prize in 1969, *Cromwell Our Chief of Men*, and *King Charles II*. She is the General Editor of the Kings and Queens of England series in which her own *King James: VI of Scotland and I of England* appeared. She has also written four mystery stories featuring Jemima Shore Investigator, now the subject of a major TV series. Antonia Fraser has edited three previous anthologies: *Scottish Love Poems* (Penguin), *Love Letters* (Penguin) and *Mary, Queen of Scots: an Anthology of Poetry* (the latter, like *Oxford in Verse*, illustrated by her daughter Rebecca).

OXFORD

and Oxfordshire

·

In Verse

·

edited and with an introduction by

ANTONIA FRASER

with the collaboration of Flora Powell-Jones
illustrations by Rebecca Fraser

Penguin Books

Penguin Books Ltd, Harmondsworth, Middlesex, England
Penguin Books, 625 Madison Avenue, New York, New York 10022, U.S.A.
Penguin Books Australia Ltd, Ringwood, Victoria, Australia
Penguin Books Canada Ltd, 2801 John Street, Markham, Ontario, Canada L3R 1B4
Penguin Books (N.Z.) Ltd, 182–190 Wairau Road, Auckland 10, New Zealand

First published by Martin Secker & Warburg Ltd 1982
Published in Penguin Books 1983

Regions in Verse series. General Editor: Emma Tennant

Made and printed in Great Britain by
Richard Clay (The Chaucer Press) Ltd, Bungay, Suffolk
Set in Monophoto Ehrhardt

For Thomas
in memory of our Centaur bikes

EDITOR'S NOTE

Many people helped me in the preparation of this book. I am particularly grateful to my daughter Flora Powell-Jones, to whose eclectic researches, carried out to commemorate the ending of her own four years at Oxford University, I owe so much. I also received valuable suggestions from the following: Anthony Astbury, as ever rich in poetical references; John Heath-Stubbs; Sally Purcell, and Anne Ridler. Lastly, my daughter Rebecca Fraser's illustrations made this a happy family affair.

CONTENTS

M: May Day, Magdalen, Martyrs' Memorial

N: Nightingales, North Oxford

O: Open Air

P: Palaces

Q: Quads

R: Rivers, Rowing, Return

S: Swimming, Spring, Spires

ACKNOWLEDGEMENTS

John Heath-Stubbs: 'Addison's Walk' from *Selected Poems* published by Oxford University Press, reprinted by permission of David Higham Associates Ltd.

Andrew Young: 'At Oxford' from *Complete Poems* reprinted by permission of Secker & Warburg Ltd.

Siegfried Sassoon: 'Sheldonian Soliloquy' reprinted by permission of George Sassoon.

Anne Ridler: Extract from 'The Golden Bird' and 'Bathing in the Windrush' from *The Golden Bird* published by Faber & Faber Ltd., reprinted by permission of Anne Ridler.

John Betjeman: 'Oxford: Sudden Illness at the Bus-stop', 'In Memory of Basil, Marquess of Dufferin and Ava' and 'May-Day Song for North Oxford' from *Collected Poems* and an extract from *Summoned by Bells* reprinted by permission of Sir John Betjeman and John Murray (Publishers) Ltd.

Ronald Arbuthnott Knox: 'The Christchurchman's Lament' and 'Megalomania' from *Juxta Salices* and 'Limerick on Idealism' reprinted by permission of the Earl of Oxford & Asquith.

Hilaire Belloc: 'Lines to a Don' from *Complete Verse* reprinted by permission of Gerald Duckworth & Co. Ltd.

Louis MacNeice: 'Autumn Journal', Canto XIII, from *The Collected Poems* reprinted by permission of Faber & Faber Ltd.

Laurence Binyon: 'Ferry Hinksey' and 'Bab-Lock-Hythe' from *Collected Poems* published by Macmillan & Co. Ltd., reprinted by permission of Mrs Nicolete Gray and The Society of Authors on behalf of the Laurence Binyon Estate.

A. L. Rowse: 'Iffley' reprinted by permission of John Johnson Ltd.

Sir Arthur Quiller-Couch: 'Behold! I am not one that goes to Lectures' reprinted by permission of Miss F. F. Quiller-Couch and Monro Pennefather & Co.

Wystan Hugh Auden: 'Oxford' and poem XXX (for Benjamin Britten) from *The English Auden* edited by Edward Mendelson, published by Faber & Faber Ltd., reprinted by permission of Curtis Brown Academic Ltd.

John Crowe Ransom: 'Philomela' from *Selected Poems* published by Eyre Methuen Ltd. and Alfred A. Knopf Inc./Random House Inc.

E. J. Scovell: 'An Open-Air Performance of *As You Like It*' from *The River Steamer* published by Barrie & Jenkins Ltd., reprinted by permission of E. J. Scovell.

David Gascoyne: 'Oxford: A Spring Day' from *Collected Poems*, © Oxford University Press 1965, reprinted by permission of Oxford University Press.

John Wain: 'Nuffield' reprinted by permission of John Wain.

Sally Purcell: 'Oxford, Early Michaelmas Term' from *The Holly Queen* published by Anvil Press Poetry, reprinted by permission of Sally Purcell.

Wilfred Rowland Childe: 'Vale' from *Selected Poems* reprinted by permission of Thomas Nelson & Sons Ltd.

Graham Greene: 'Sonnet' from *Oxford Poetry* edited by P. Monkhouse and C. Plumb, published by Basil Blackwell, reprinted by permission of Graham Greene.

Max Beerbohm: 'To an Undergraduate Needing Rooms in Oxford' from the novel *Zuleika Dobson* published by William Heinemann Ltd., reprinted by permission of Mrs Eva Reichmann.

INTRODUCTION

I cannot remember the time before I lived in Oxford (although I was born in London). I can also hardly remember the time before I read poetry – aloud and to myself. I read it aloud because I took it for granted that was how you read poetry and I read it alone because I quickly discovered reading poetry to be a secret pleasure, intoxicating myself with words in private; however, I don't remember many family complaints about my decision.

The first book of poetry I actually owned, Palgrave's *Golden Treasury*, was given to me by my father. I inscribed it at once: 'Antonia Pakenham, 8 Chadlington Road, Oxford, Oxfordshire, England, Britain, Europe, The World, The Universe.' The second, *The Dragon Book of Verse*, was presented to me, aged eight, on my first day at the eponymous Dragon School, and was similarly inscribed. I added: 'Black is the raven, black is the rook, but blacker the person who stealeth this book.' Either the impressive address or the dire admonition has protected these two books down the ages. While the loved books of my adolescence are lost, I still possess them both. Oxford and poetry are thus inseparably entwined in my recollections, and like these two books, will doubtless remain there, enshrined, long after other later memories have vanished.

The poems I have chosen make up the images of my Oxford past, arranged alphabetically – by image, not author's name. In other words, here are poems from Adlestrop to Zuleika. After all, does not Adlestrop generously embrace all the birds of Oxfordshire in its last line? As for the Duke of Dorset's poem from *Zuleika Dobson*, is it not subtitled, 'Sonnet in Oxfordshire Dialect'? Even if Max Beerbohm added with some truth, 'His was not a Muse that could with a good grace doff the grand manner.'

It was not, however, for the sake of fulfilling this particular alphabetical fantasy that I chose the arrangement in the first place, although I must admit that I found the Adlestrop-Zuleika conjunction irresistible. I was anxious to avoid the rigidity of the chronological approach. Essential perhaps for more orthodox anthologies, this kind of listing has never produced for me such exciting results as arrangement according to the editor's personal predilection, when unusual juxtapositions enable one to make fresh discoveries, feel fresh emotions aroused by even the best-known poems.

These, then, are the images which swirl about my head when I think of Oxford, settling like a kaleidoscope, now in one pattern, now in another. After completing the anthology, I found that when I recited all the names together – aloud, as in the days of yore – I had created my own kind of Oxford and Oxfordshire rune, a sort of stream of past consciousness. Thus: 'Adlestrop, August, Addison's Walk, Academics . . . Bells, Birds, Botanical Gardens, Bodleian, Binsey, Bicycles . . . Cherwell, Canal, Christ Church, Commem . . .' But this is to anticipate.

First – before the war – there was Singletree, Rose Hill, on the Iffley Road going out of South Oxford. It was a geographical location dictated, we were told, by our father's political ambitions: Rose Hill was convenient for the Morris Oxford (Nuffield) car works, where sympathetic Labour voters were to be found. Nowadays Nuffield's products make this district unrecognizable with traffic, although the street names are unchanged: as John Wain writes, 'Shrouded in pastoral names/(Rose Hill and Blackbird Leys) the world he killed/Mocks us.' In those days Rose Hill to the country was only five pram's minutes away.

This was the Iffley of A. L. Rowse's poem:

The almond-trees are out in flower,
The water plashes from the weir
A softer music: the year was young
When you were here, when you were here.

My brother Thomas and I like Rowse's year were young, and our favourite walk was to Iffley Lock. Here, gazing at the obedient river altering its level to the lock-keeper's commands, we encountered the first of many Oxford waters. 'Cherwell' (Thomas Warton's eighteenth century *Complaint*) . . . 'Isis' (a sonnet by Wordsworth) . . . 'Swimming' (Anne Ridler's *Bathing in the Windrush*) . . . 'Thames' (Thomas Love Peacock's *The Genius of the Thames*): it is no coincidence that so many of the images prove to be of water since for many years the river, propulsion along it or immersion in it, dominated my life.

The first play I ever saw dates from this time – *The Tempest*, outdoors in Worcester Gardens, with, as I recall, a real boat getting wrecked on the lake and certainly some real-life rain for the storm (which you could probably count on during June in Oxford and have as part of the stage directions). E. J. Scovell's *An Open-Air Performance of 'As You Like It'* refers movingly and with approval to the 'soft and stubborn questions' of children on a similar occasion: I am not sure that Thomas and I met with similar tolerance. Perhaps our questions were not stubborn (or not soft) enough.

At the beginning of the war, when I was seven and Thomas six, we changed Oxfordshire direction completely. We went to live in an Elizabethan manor called Water Eaton, lying on the (mainly flooded, not so obedient) river to the north of Oxford, in the Banbury direction: a kind of evacuation since the hospitable family who owned the house had decided to take in two other families, both with children. It was at Water Eaton Manor, with its dark wooden panelling, its mullioned windows, its priest's hidey-hole, even the deep chill of its stone interiors, that I discovered the romantic – which meant tragic – history I loved, come to life. There was Woodstock nearby, the scene of Fair Rosamund's grisly encounter with Queen Eleanor, here described in W. B. Scott's *Woodstock Maze*. Of course when at Woodstock I much preferred to dwell on Fair Rosamund's story than on that of the Duke of Marlborough; like Pope 'the grand approach' of Blenheim Palace was not altogether to my taste.

We also used to visit Cumnor, a few miles from Oxford: as a result I had become obsessed with the story of Amy Robsart, found lying like a heap of swan's feathers at the bottom of the Cumnor Hall oubliette, in Scott's *Kenilworth*. What of similar tragedy might not befall me at Water Eaton . . .? W. J. Mickle's ballad, quoted by Scott in the introduction to his book, commemorates these forebodings:

And ere the dawn of day appear'd
In Cumnor Hall, so lone and drear,
Full many a piercing scream was heard,
And many a cry of mortal fear.

The tragedy which did befall us was having to leave Water Eaton after a year and settle down to being dons' children in North Oxford, riding bicycles and attending the Dragon School, like everyone else of this particular breed. I was, however, very happy at the Dragon School, nor did life there separate me from poetry. On the contrary, poetry, like everything else, was seen in exhilaratingly competitive terms at the Dragon School. In the frequent end-of-term competitions for who could recite loudest, clearest and above all longest from *The Dragon Book of Verse*, I was naturally to the fore.

John Betjeman is the bard of North Oxford, as of so many other things: be it 'Take me, my Centaur bike, down Linton Road,' or 'Belbroughton Road is bonny, and pinkly bursts the spray', his poems are the maps of my childhood. But I have also included his lines to a don's wife, not only to atone for two attacks on dons – Dr Fell and Chesterton's unwise critic, savaged by Belloc – but also because dons' wives such as my mother and Billa Harrod are quite as much part of the images of my youth as their husbands, the dons, if not more so. The latter were, after all, frequently absent at something called High Table, evidently far too high above the heads of us children (and for that matter of their wives) for them to be generally visible.

My father, invalided out of the army, returned to his peacetime profession as a don at Christ Church. Here the average temperature of his rooms in Tom Quad, even before the war, had caused us children to prefer the raw winter air. Tom Quad itself, though, we thought very fine and Bishop Corbet's poem to Great Tom commemorates the Christ Church bells. In wartime, the bells fell silent, yet enough of bells, both before and after the war, remains ding-donged into my memory for me to agree with the Rev. James Hurdis, an eighteenth century Professor of Poetry, that any bell, anywhere in the world, immediately brings back Oxford.

> I ask not for the cause – it matters not.
> It is enough for me to hear the sound
> Of the remote exhilarating peal,
> Now dying all away, now faintly heard . . .

And then there was Oxfordshire, by no means so divided from the town as it is now. On our Centaur bikes Thomas and I duly achieved Binsey, Bagley Woods, Hinksey, Marston, Elsfield, Charlton and even Dorchester – the latter a disastrous camping expedition which bore little relation to William Morris' romantic foray there, here included under the image of 'August'. The month itself is also an important image to me in its own right, since our summer holidays were spent in Oxford, and I have always retained great affection for the dusty August city, extra-lethargic cricket on the browning grass of the University Parks, undergraduates fled, only bewildered tourists wandering in the quads.

William Morris' lines:

Ah, love! such happy days, such days as these,
Must we still waste them, craving for the best . . .

are on the other hand more appropriate to my subsequent experience at the University itself. My years spent studying history there are probably best summed up by the three images 'Learning, Lectures, Love' – especially if the first line of Quiller-Couch's brilliant parody of Walt Whitman is borne in mind:

Behold! I am not one that goes to Lectures . . .

Of the two poems I have included under 'Love', one is by W. H. Auden, my favourite poet when I was at Oxford. It is one of my favourite love poems now:

Underneath the abject willow,
Lover, sulk no more;
Act from thought should quickly follow:
What is thinking for?

The other is about love *for* Oxford by Gerard Manley Hopkins, one of my favourite poets now, as this is my favourite Oxford poem.

Neither is exactly about the radiant satisfaction of requited love while at University but that is appropriate enough. I don't remember being radiant about anything very much while at Oxford.

> I was so happy to that Ford I came,
> Which of the labouring Ox doth bear the name.

Alas, the seventeenth-century sentiments of George Wither were seldom mine.

Perhaps I had been spoilt by my Oxford childhood. Coming up to Lady Margaret Hall, I could never feel, as Sally Purcell expresses it in *Oxford, Early Michaelmas Term*, 'delight in imagined possession/of the inherited magic world' – for hadn't I inherited it, the daughter of Academe, many years earlier? Perhaps it was merely a case of something universal known as 'Youth', of being, in the words of Graham Greene's sonnet: 'Fearful of peace, more fearful still of action,/Fighting beneath no banner, with no song.' A more characteristic experience than feeling delight for me while an undergraduate was to seek out the Oxford Canal. Most members of the University never even knew it existed, and I would walk up and down its banks in delicious lonely morbidity. It is an experience perfectly evoked by James Elroy Flecker's poem:

> When you have wearied of the valiant spires of this County Town,
> Of its wide white streets and glistening museums, and black monastic
>   walls,
> Of its red motors and lumbering trams, and self-sufficient people,
> I will take you walking with me to a place you have not seen –
> Half town and half country – the land of the Canal.

At least the river was still there: the Cherwell which had flowed past Water Eaton, past at the bottom of our Chadlington Road garden, past the Dragon School playing-fields, now bordered the gardens of Lady Margaret Hall. Robert Bridges' *A Water-Party* and above all Laurence Binyon's *Bab-Lock-Hythe* – 'In the time of wild roses/As up the Thames we travelled' – recreated for me what in retrospect seem my happiest moments at Oxford.

Lastly, 'Return' and 'Vale' remain important images for all where Oxford is concerned. I freely confess that for all the above megrims, I have done a great deal more Return-ing than Vale-ing, in the thirty odd years since I left Oxford theoretically for good. 'Too rare, too rare, grow now my visits here' cries Mathew Arnold in *Thyrsis* (the poem in which Oxford was first christened 'that sweet city with her dreaming spires'). I can scarcely echo his complaint. Research of my own in the Bodleian Library, visits to a daughter at the University, even some bizarre combination of the two, such as a visit to the daughter doing research *in* the Bodleian Library, any improbable excuse will do to turn up, as everyone who has ever shared the nostalgia well knows.

These poems too are chosen so that I can put in a humble claim to Oxford, or at least to my own past within it, using the words of Gerard Manley Hopkins, and of many other poets both living and dead: 'This is my park, my pleasaunce . . .'

Antonia Fraser

The Sheldonian, Oxford

EDWARD THOMAS
[1878–1917]

Adlestrop

Yes. I remember Adlestrop –
The name, because one afternoon
Of heat the express-train drew up there
Unwontedly. It was late June.

The steam hissed. Someone cleared his throat.
No one left and no one came
On the bare platform. What I saw
Was Adlestrop – only the name

And willows, willow-herb, and grass,
And meadowsweet, and haycocks dry,
No whit less still and lonely fair
Than the high cloudlets in the sky.

And for that minute a blackbird sang
Close by, and round him, mistier,
Farther and farther, all the birds
Of Oxfordshire and Gloucestershire.

WILLIAM MORRIS
[1834–1896]

August
from 'The Earthly Paradise'

Across the gap made by our English hinds,
Amidst the Roman's handiwork, behold
Far off the long-roofed church; the shepherd binds
The withy round the hurdles of his fold,
Down in the foss the river fed of old,
That through long lapse of time has grown to be
The little grassy valley that you see.

Rest here awhile, not yet the eve is still,
The bees are wandering yet, and you may hear
The barley mowers on the trenchéd hill,
The sheep-bells, and the restless changing weir,
All little sounds made musical and clear
Beneath the sky that burning August gives,
While yet the thought of glorious Summer lives.

Ah, love! such happy days, such days as these,
Must we still waste them, craving for the best,
Like lovers o'er the painted images
Of those who once their yearning hearts have blessed?
Have we been happy on our day of rest?
Thine eyes say 'yes,' – but if it came again,
Perchance its ending would not seem so vain.

Now came fulfilment of the year's desire,
The tall wheat, coloured by the August fire
Grew heavy-headed, dreading its decay,
And blacker grew the elm-trees day by day.
About the edges of the yellow corn,
And o'er the gardens grown somewhat outworn
The bees went hurrying to fill up their store;
The apple-boughs bent over more and more;

With peach and apricot the garden wall
Was odorous, and the pears began to fall
From off the high tree with each freshening breeze.

So in a house bordered about with trees,
A little raised above the waving gold
The Wanderers heard this marvellous story told,
While 'twixt the gleaming flasks of ancient wine,
They watched the reapers' slow advancing line.

JOHN HEATH-STUBBS
[b. 1918]

Addison's Walk
from 'The Heart's Forest'

Grove, and you, trees, by careless birds
   Frequented, and you fronds, impersonal,
   Whose greenness soothed the long intestine broil
   Within my head, when I would seek your shades

Those former months of solitude, remembering
   That sane cool mind who christened you, quietly,
   In his discreet and formal century
   Beside the unhurried river's marge walking;

Now that together in the season's prime
   We've come this way, marked the symbolic flowers,
   And the axe striking on the murdered willows,

When this is over, and the wing of time
   Has brushed aside desire, in after years
   Returning here, what ghosts will haunt these shadows?

ANDREW YOUNG
[1885–1971]

At Oxford

Though cold December rains draw vanishing rings
    On the choked Isis that goes swirling by,
These academic gowns flap like the wings
    Of half-fledged blackbirds that attempt to fly.

RICHARD, BISHOP CORBET
[1582–1635]

Great Tom

Be dumb ye infant chimes, thump not the metal
That ne'er outrung a tinker and his kettle,
Cease all your petty larums, for to-day
Is young Tom's resurrection from the clay:
And know, when Tom shall ring his loudest knells
The big'st of you'll be thought but dinner bells . . .
Rejoice with Christ Church – look higher Oseney,
Of giant bells the famous treasury;
The base vast thundering Clock of Westminster,
Grave Tom of Lincoln and huge Excester
Are but Tom's eldest brothers, and perchance
He may call cousin with the bell of France.

REV. JAMES HURDIS
[1763–1801]

from *The Village Curate*

Then let the village bells, as often wont,
Come swelling on the breeze, and to the sun,
Half-set, sing merrily their ev'ning song.
I ask not for the cause – it matters not.
It is enough for me to hear the sound
Of the remote exhilarating peal,
Now dying all away, now faintly heard,
And now with loud and musical relapse
Its mellow changes huddling on the ear.
So have I stood at eve on Isis' banks,
To hear the merry Christ-Church bells rejoice.
So have I sat too in thy honour'd shades,
Distinguish'd Magdalen, on Cherwell's brink,
To hear thy silver Wolsey tones so sweet.
And so too have I paus'd and held my oar,
And suffer'd the slow stream to bear me home,
While Wykeham's peal along the meadow ran.

SIEGFRIED SASSOON
[1886–1967]

Sheldonian Soliloquy
(During Bach's B Minor Mass)

My music-loving Self this afternoon
(Clothed in the gilded surname of Sassoon)
Squats in the packed Sheldonian and observes
An intellectual bee-hive perched and seated
In achromatic and expectant curves
Of buzzing, sunbeam-flecked, and overheated
Accommodation. Skins perspire . . . But hark! . . .
Begins the great *B minor Mass* of Bach.

The choir sings *Gloria in excelsis Deo*
With confident and well-conducted *brio*.
Outside, a motor-bike makes impious clatter,
Impinging on our Eighteenth-Century trammels.
God's periwigged: He takes a pinch of snuff.
The music's half-rococo . . . Does it matter
While those intense musicians shout the stuff
In Catholic Latin to the cultured mammals
Who agitate the pages of their scores? . . .

Meanwhile, in Oxford sunshine out of doors,
Birds in collegiate gardens rhapsodize
Antediluvian airs of worm-thanksgiving.
To them the austere and buried Bach replies
With song that from ecclesiasmus cries
Eternal *Resurrexit* to the living.

Hosanna in excelsis chants the choir
In pious contrapuntal jubilee.
Hosanna shrill the birds in sunset fire.
And Benedictus sings my heart to Me.

ANNE RIDLER
[b. 1912]

Pegasus in the Botanical Gardens
from 'The Golden Bird'

So we came . . .
To a place where three ways and two seasons met,
In spring at the edge of Oxford.

'Here,' said the Fox, 'is a city of screaming tyres,
Where lorries piled with motor-shells
Fly like clumsy Maybugs through the streets,
And the river drumbles past exotic barges.
The smoke of learning rises with the river-mists
And spires like funnels carry praise to heaven.
Thin and rare is the rising praise
But the heavenly thought descends in flesh and blood.
Once with tremendous wings vanning the sky
It seemed a flying horse, and prayed for, came
To kill the chimaera of men's dismal fears;
Then sprang, like a diver rising from the depths, to Olympus,
Throwing its rider, who would have ridden to heaven
But had not learnt its horsemanship . . .'

I crossed the bridge, with the whirling wrack of traffic.
The sky was laid below me in azure anemones,
The willows wept against the sun like rainbows
And punts as lazy as clouds slipped by beneath.
I came to the double gateway
Where the Stuarts guard the tranquil garden,
The chimes fall among rare plants like rain
And blackened ashlar walls debar
The rabble of 'prams and all disorderly persons'.
A wolf and boar of stone
Sat snarling back on their haunches,
And the Horse of the wind-outpacing thought
Quietly fed there, tasting
The luculent waxen blooms
Of the leafless magnolia tree.

THOMAS TICKELL
[1686–1740]

from *Oxford*

Next let the Muse record our Bodley's seat,
Nor aim at numbers like the subject great.
All hail! thou fabric sacred to the Nine,
Thy fame immortal and thy form divine!
Who to thy praise attempts the dangerous flight
Should in thy various tongues be taught to write;
His verse, like thee, a lofty dress should wear,
And breathe the genius which inhabits there;
Thy proper lays alone can make thee live,
And pay that fame which first thyself did give:
So fountains which through secret channels flow,
And pour above, the floods they take below,
Back to their father Ocean urge their way,
And to the sea the streams it gave repay.

No more we fear the military rage
Nurs'd up in some obscure barbarian age,
Nor dread the ruin of our arts divine
From thick-skull'd heroes of the gothic line,
Though pale the Romans saw those arms advance,
And wept their learning lost in ignorance.
Let brutal rage around its terrors spread,
The living murder, and consume the dead,
In impious fires let noblest writings burn,
And, with their authors, share a common urn,
Only, ye fates! our lov'd Bodleian spare,
Be It, and Learning's self shall be, your care;

GERARD MANLEY HOPKINS
[1844–1889]

Binsey Poplars
felled 1879

My aspens dear, whose airy cages quelled,
Quelled or quenched in leaves the leaping sun,
All felled, felled, are all felled;
   Of a fresh and following folded rank
      Not spared, not one
      That dandled a sandalled
    Shadow that swam or sank
On meadow and river and wind-wandering
   weed-winding bank.

  O if we but knew what we do
     When we delve or hew –
    Hack and rack the growing green!
      Since country is so tender
    To touch, her being só slender,
    That, like this sleek and seeing ball
    But a prick will make no eye at all,

   Where we, even where we mean
      To mend her we end her,
    When we hew or delve:
After-comers cannot guess the beauty been.
  Ten or twelve, only ten or twelve
    Strokes of havoc únselve
     The sweet especial scene,
  Rural scene, a rural scene,
  Sweet especial rural scene.

JOHN BETJEMAN
[b. 1906]

from *'Summoned by Bells'*

Take me, my Centaur bike, down Linton Road,
Gliding by newly planted almond trees
Where the young dons with wives in tussore clad
Were building in the morning of their lives
Houses for future Dragons. Rest an arm
Upon the post of the allotment path,
Then dare the slope! We choked in our own dust,
The narrowness of the footpath made our speed
Seem swift as light. May-bush and elm flashed by,
Allotment holders turning round to stare,
Potatoes in their hands. Speed-wobble! Help!
And, with the Sturmey-Archer three-speed gear
Safely in bottom, resting from the race
We pedalled round the new-mown meadow-grass
By Marston Ferry with its punt and chain.
    Show me thy road, Crick, in the early spring:
Laurel and privet and laburnum ropes
And gabled-gothic houses gathered round
Thy mothering spire, St Philip and St James.
Here by the low brick semi-private walls
Bicycling past a trotting butcher's-cart,
I glimpsed, behind lace curtains, silver hair
Of sundry old Professors. Here were friends
Of Ruskin, Newman, Pattison and Froude
Among their books and plants and photographs
In comfortable twilight. But for me,
Less academic, red-brick Chalfont Road
Meant great-aunt Wilkins, tea and buttered toast.

THOMAS WARTON
[1728–1790]

from *'Ode IX: The Complaint of Cherwell'*

I

All penſive from her oſier-woven bow'r
CHERWELL aroſe. Around her darkening edge
Park Eve began the ſteaming miſt to pour,
And breezes fann'd by fits the ruſtling ſedge;
She roſe, and thus ſhe cried in deep deſpair,
And tore the ruſhy wreath that bound her ſtreaming hair.

II

Ah! why, ſhe cried, ſhould Isis ſhare alone
The tributary gifts of tuneful fame!
Shall every ſong her happier influence own,
And ſtamp with partial praiſe her favorite name?
While I, alike to thoſe proud domes allied,
Nor hear the Muſe's call, nor boaſt a claſſic tide.

III

No choſen ſon of all yon ſabling band
Bids my looſe locks their gloſſy length diffuſe;
Nor ſees my coral-cinctur'd ſtole expand
Its folds, beſprent with Spring's unnumber'd hues:
No poet builds my grotto's dripping cell,
Nor ſtuds my cryſtal throne with many a ſpeckled ſhell.

IV

In Isis' vaſe if Fancy's eye diſcern
Majeſtic towers emboſs'd in ſculpture high;
Lo! milder glories mark my modeſt urn,
The ſimple ſcenes of paſtoral imagery:
What though ſhe pace ſublime, a ſtately queen?
Mine is the gentle grace, the meek retiring mien.

JAMES ELROY FLECKER
[1884–1915]

Oxford Canal

When you have wearied of the valiant spires of this County Town,
Of its wide white streets and glistening museums, and black monastic walls,
Of its red motors and lumbering trams, and self-sufficient people,
I will take you walking with me to a place you have not seen –
Half town and half country – the land of the Canal.
It is dearer to me than the antique town: I love it more than the rounded hills:
Straightest, sublimest of rivers is the long Canal.
I have observed great storms and trembled: I have wept for fear of the dark.
But nothing makes me so afraid as the clear water of this idle canal on a summer's noon.
Do you see the great telephone poles down in the water, how every wire is distinct?
If a body fell into the canal it would rest entangled in those wires for ever, between earth and air.
For the water is as deep as the stars are high.
One day I was thinking how if a man fell from that lofty pole
He would rush through the water toward me till his image was scattered by his splash,
When suddenly a train rushed by: the brazen dome of the engine flashed: the long white carriages roared;
The sun veiled himself for a moment, and the signals loomed in fog;
A savage woman screamed at me from a barge: little children began to cry;
The untidy landscape rose to life; a sawmill started;
A cart rattled down to the wharf, and workmen clanged over the iron footbridge;
A beautiful old man nodded from the first story window of a square red house,
And a pretty girl came out to hang up clothes in a small delightful garden.

O strange motion in the suburb of a county town: slow regular movement of the dance of death!

Men and not phantoms are these that move in light.

Forgotten they live, and forgotten die.

RONALD ARBUTHNOTT KNOX
[1888–1957]

The Christchurchman's Lament

[Being some account of the motives which induced certain
gentlemen to set fire to the Stand designed for the
Oxford Pageant of 1907.]
   (With occasional apologies to MATTHEW ARNOLD.)

THE CHRISTCHURCHMAN *loquitur:—*

How changed is every spot man makes, or unmakes!
   In Northern Oxford nothing keeps the same,
And here, in Christ Church meadows, where the sun makes
   The Cher in summer worthy of its name,
A mushroom growth, raised by a local agent,
   A mighty platform threatens the display
Which uninstructed people call a pageant
   (Though that, I think, is not the proper way).

Ladies, that punt beneath the cool-haired creepers,
   Each clutching her inviolable shade,
Fail to observe the customary reapers
   Stand with suspended scythe in yonder glade;
Women they see, their hands upraised in cursing,
   Like Suffragists, beneath the eye of Heaven,
And these, they know, are characters rehearsing
   The culminating scene in Tableau VII.

Bumpkins, that came to hear the choir-boys carol
   From Magdalen Tower on May-day, stood and roared
To see strange men in latter-day apparel
   March with umbrellas o'er the trampled sward:
Perhaps those serried companies presented
   The loyal muster of King Charles's men,
Perhaps, how undergraduates frequented
   Lectures – ah yes! they still had lectures then.

Fain had I lived when Aelfred burnt the crumpets,
   Ere Oxford knew the guile that haunts the gown,
Or when the sudden blare of Roundhead trumpets
   Would send a proctor flying round the town;
Or when the Magdalen fellows, rusticated,
   Begged their precarious bread o'er lawn and lea,
Then, harmless Indolence was never 'gated,' –
   But Time, not Indolence, has done for me.

Come, cross, my friends, the unpermitted ferry;
   Soon from the High will firemen's pumps come on;
Soon we shall have the Oxford coster merry
   Charging us, here a bobby, there a don;
Achilles in his tent, the pageant-master
   Shall see young Hectors raising brands on high,
And cease his boding presage of disaster.
   Commem. is come, and with Commem. come I.

                [He plunges into the Cherwell.]

THOMAS BROWN
[1663–1704]

Dr Fell

I do not love you, Dr Fell,
But why I cannot tell;
But this I know full well,
I do not love you, Dr Fell.

(adaptation of an Epigram by Martial to Satidius)

Dean of Christ Church from 1660 and Bishop of Oxford 1676, John Fell occasioned these verses from Thomas Brown, an undergraduate from 1678–82.

HILAIRE BELLOC
[1870–1953]

from *Lines to a Don*

Remote and ineffectual Don
That dared attack my Chesterton,
With that poor weapon, half-impelled,
Unlearnt, unsteady, hardly held,
Unworthy for a tilt with men –
Your quavering and corroded pen;
Don poor at Bed and worse at Table,
Don pinched, Don starved, Don miserable;
Don stuttering, Don with roving eyes,
Don nervous, Don of crudities;
Don clerical, Don ordinary,
Don self-absorbed and solitary;
Don here-and-there, Don epileptic;
Don puffed and empty, Don dyspeptic;
Don middle-class, Don sycophantic,
Don dull, Don brutish, Don pedantic;
Don hypocritical, Don bad,
Don furtive, Don three-quarters mad;
Don (since a man must make an end),
Don that shall never be my friend.

Don very much apart from these,
Thou scapegoat Don, thou Don devoted,
Don to thine own damnation quoted,
Perplexed to find thy trivial name
Reared in my verse to lasting shame.
Don dreadful, rasping Don and wearing,
Repulsive Don – Don past all bearing.
Don of the cold and doubtful breath,
Don despicable, Don of death;
Don nasty, skimpy, silent, level;
Don evil; Don that serves the devil.
Don ugly – that makes fifty lines.

There is a Canon which confines
A Rhymed Octosyllabic Curse
If written in Iambic Verse
To fifty lines. I never cut;
I far prefer to end it – but
Believe me I shall soon return.
My fires are banked, but still they burn
To write some more about the Don
That dared attack my Chesterton.

Lines to a don

JOHN BETJEMAN
[b. 1906]

Oxford: Sudden Illness at the Bus-stop

At the time of evening when cars run sweetly,
  Syringas blossom by Oxford gates.
In her evening velvet with a rose pinned neatly
  By the distant bus-stop a don's wife waits.

From that wide bedroom with its two branched lighting
  Over her looking-glass, up or down,
When sugar was short and the world was fighting
  She first appeared in that velvet gown.

What forks since then have been slammed in places?
  What peas turned out from how many a tin?
From plate-glass windows how many faces
  Have watched professors come hobbling in?

Too much, too many! so fetch the doctor,
  This dress has grown such a heavier load
Since Jack was only a Junior Proctor,
  And rents were lower in Rawlinson Road.

GERARD MANLEY HOPKINS
[1844–1889]

Duns Scotus's Oxford

Towery city and branchy between towers;
Cuckoo-echoing, bell-swarmèd, lark-charmèd, rook-racked, river-
   rounded;
The dapple-eared lily below thee; that country and town did
Once encounter in, here coped and poisèd powers.

Thou hast a base and brickish skirt there, sours
That neighbour-nature thy grey beauty is grounded
Best in; graceless growth, thou hast confounded
Rural rural keeping – folk, flocks, and flowers.

Yet ah! this air I gather and I release
He lived on; these weeds and waters, these walls are what
He haunted who of all men most sways my spirits to peace;

Of realty the rarest-veinèd unraveller; a not
Rivalled insight, be rival Italy or Greece;
Who fired France for Mary without spot.

LOUIS MACNEICE
[1907–1963]

Autumn Journal, Canto XIII

Which things being so, as we said when we studied
    The classics, I ought to be glad
That I studied the classics at Marlborough and Merton,
    Not everyone here having had
The privilege of learning a language
    That is incontrovertibly dead,
And of carting a toy-box of hall-marked marmoreal phrases
    Around in his head.
We wrote compositions in Greek which they said was a lesson
    In logic and good for the brain;
We marched, counter-marched to the field-marshal's blue-pencil
      baton,
    We dressed by the right and we wrote out the sentence again.
We learned that a gentleman never misplaces his accents,
    That nobody knows how to speak, much less how to write
English who has not hob-nobbed with the great-grand-parents of
      English,
    That the boy on the Modern Side is merely a parasite
But the classical student is bred to the purple, his training in syntax
    Is also a training in thought
And even in morals; if called to the bar or the barracks
    He always will do what he ought.
And knowledge, besides, should be prized for the sake of knowledge:
    Oxford crowded the mantelpiece with gods –
Scaliger, Heinsius, Dindorf, Bentley and Wilamowitz –
    As we learned our genuflexions for Honour Mods.
And then they taught us philosophy, logic and metaphysics,
    The Negative Judgment and the Ding an Sich,
And every single thinker was powerful as Napoleon
    And crafty as Metternich.
And it really was very attractive to be able to talk about tables
    And to ask if the table *is*,
And to draw the cork out of an old conundrum
    And watch the paradoxes fizz.

And it made one confident to think that nothing
    Really was what it seemed under the sun,
That the actual was not real and the real was not with us
    And all that mattered was the One.
And they said 'The man in the street is so naïve, he never
    Can see the wood for the trees;
He thinks he knows he sees a thing but cannot
    Tell you how he knows the thing he thinks he sees.'
And oh how much I liked the Concrete Universal,
    I never thought that I should
Be telling them vice-versa
    That they can't see the trees for the wood.
But certainly it was fun while it lasted
    And I got my honours degree
And was stamped as a person of intelligence and culture
    For ever wherever two or three
Persons of intelligence and culture
    Are gathered together in talk
Writing definitions on invisible blackboards
    In non-existent chalk.
But such sacramental occasions
    Are nowadays comparatively rare;
There is always a wife or a boss or a dun or a client
    Disturbing the air.
Barbarians always, life in the particular always,
    Dozens of men in the street,
And the perennial if unimportant problem
    Of getting enough to eat.
So blow the bugles over the metaphysicians,
    Let the pure mind return to the Pure Mind;
I must be content to remain in the world of Appearance
    And sit on the mere appearance of a behind.
But in case you should think my education was wasted
    I hasten to explain
That having once been to the University of Oxford
    You can never really again

Believe anything that anyone says and that of course is an asset
    In a world like ours;
Why bother to water a garden
    That is planted with paper flowers?
O the Freedom of the Press, the Late Night Final,
    To-morrow's pulp;
One should not gulp one's port but as it isn't
    Port, I'll gulp it if I want to gulp
But probably I'll just enjoy the colour
    And pour it down the sink
For I don't call advertisement a statement
    Or any quack medicine a drink.
Good-bye now, Plato and Hegel,
    The shop is closing down;
They don't want any philosopher-kings in England,
    There ain't no universals in this man's town.

JOHN BETJEMAN
[b. 1906]

In Memory of Basil,
Marquess of Dufferin and Ava

On such a morning as this
  with the birds ricocheting their music
Out of the whelming elms
  to a copper beech's embrace
And a sifting sound of leaves
  from multitudinous branches
Running across the park
  to a chequer of light on the lake,
On such a morning as this
  with *The Times* for June the eleventh
Left with coffee and toast
  you opened the breakfast-room window
And, sprawled on the southward terrace,
  Said: 'That means war in September.'

Friend of my youth, you are dead!
  and the long peal pours from the steeple
Over this sunlit quad
  in our University city
And soaks in Headington stone.
  Motionless stand the pinnacles.
Under a flying sky
  as though they too listened and waited
Like me for your dear return
  with a Bullingdon noise of an evening
In a Sports-Bugatti from Thame
  that belonged to a man in Magdalen.
Friend of my youth, you are dead!
  and the quads are empty without you.

Then there were people about.
   Each hour, like an Oxford archway,
Opened on long green lawns
   and distant unvisited buildings
And you my friend were explorer
   and so you remained to me always
Humorous, reckless, loyal –
   my kind, heavy-lidded companion.
Stop, oh many bells, stop
   pouring on roses and creeper
Your unremembering peal
   this hollow, unhallowed V.E. day, –
I am deaf to your notes and dead
   by a soldier's body in Burma.

WILLIAM WORDSWORTH
[1770–1850]

A Parsonage in Oxfordshire

Where holy ground begins, unhallowed ends,
Is marked by no distinguishable line;
The turf unites, the pathways intertwine;
And, wheresoe'er the stealing footstep tends,
Garden, and that Domain where kindred, friends,
And neighbours rest together, here confound
Their several features, mingled like the sound
Of many waters, or as evening blends
With shady night. Soft airs, from shrub and flower,
Waft fragrant greetings to each silent grave;
And while those lofty poplars gently wave
Their tops, between them comes and goes a sky
Bright as the glimpses of eternity,
To saints accorded in their mortal hour.

LAURENCE BINYON
[1869–1943]

Ferry Hinksey

Beyond the ferry water
That fast and silent flowed,
She turned, she gazed a moment,
Then took her onward road

Between the winding willows
To a city white with spires:
It seemed a path of pilgrims
To the home of earth's desires.

Blue shade of golden branches
Spread for her journeying,
Till he that lingered lost her
Among the leaves of Spring.

WILLIAM WORDSWORTH
[1770–1850]

Oxford, May 30, 1820

Ye sacred Nurseries of blooming Youth!
In whose collegiate shelter England's Flowers
Expand, enjoying through their vernal hours
The air of liberty, the light of truth;
Much have ye suffered from Time's gnawing tooth:
Yet, O ye spires of Oxford! domes and towers!
Gardens and groves! your presence overpowers
The soberness of reason; till, in sooth,
Transformed, and rushing on a bold exchange,
I slight my own beloved Cam, to range
Where silver Isis leads my stripling feet;
Pace the long avenue, or glide adown
The stream-like windings of that glorious street –
An eager Novice robed in fluttering gown!

A. L. ROWSE
[b. 1903]

Iffley

The shadows on the Norman tower
   Make clearer still the vivid day;
They write their living signature
   On all that stands, and go their way:

Images of Time that moves,
   Touching with tip of careless wing
The subtle fabric of our loves
   Silencing the hearts that sing.

The almond-trees are out in flower,
   The water plashes from the weir
A softer music: the year was young
   When you were here, when you were here.

The villas on the river bank
   Look gaily down their verdant slopes;
The quiet anglers cast their line;
   Against the wall the water laps.

Over the meadows the floods are out,
   A silver shield upon the mere
Burns and dazzles the winter eye:
   Islands of green and blue appear,

A fringe of snow-white gulls, a swan
   Sailing the blue and silver flood
That drowns the plain: the placid lake
   Reflects Boars Hill and Bagley Wood.

A distant drone of aeroplanes;
   The barges corrugate the stream,
The aspiring poplars shimmer and sway;
   The click of the gate disturbs my dream –

And I remember when you were here:
  Something has gone from the living day
With the shifting shadows upon the tower,
  Now you're away, now you're away.

WILLIAM MORRIS
[1834–1896]

June
from 'The Earthly Paradise'

O June, O June, that we desired so,
　　Wilt thou not make us happy on this day?
Across the river thy soft breezes blow
Sweet with the scent of beanfields far away,
Above our heads rustle the aspens grey,
Calm is the sky with harmless clouds beset,
No thought of storm the morning vexes yet.

　　See, we have left our hopes and fears behind
To give our very hearts up unto thee;
What better place than this then could we find
By this sweet stream that knows not of the sea,
That guesses not the city's misery,
This little stream whose hamlets scarce have names,
This far-off, lonely mother of the Thames?

　　Here then, O June, thy kindness will we take;
And if indeed but pensive men we seem,
What should we do? thou wouldst not have us wake
From out the arms of this rare happy dream
And wish to leave the murmur of the stream,
The rustling boughs, the twitter of the birds,
And all thy thousand peaceful happy words.

Now in the early June they deemed it good
That they should go unto a house that stood
On their chief river, so upon a day
With favouring wind and tide they took their way
Up the fair stream; most lovely was the time
Even amidst the days of that fair clime,
And still the wanderers thought about their lives,
And that desire that rippling water gives

To youthful hearts to wander anywhere.
   So midst sweet sights and sounds a house most fair
They came to, set upon the river side
Where kindly folk their coming did abide;
There they took land, and in the lime-trees' shade
Beneath the trees they found the fair feast laid,
And sat, well pleased; but when the water-hen
Had got at last to think them harmless men,
And they with rest, and pleasure, and old wine,
Began to feel immortal and divine,
An elder spoke, 'O gentle friends, the day
Amid such calm delight now slips away,
And ye yourselves are grown so bright and glad
I care not if I tell you something sad;
Sad, though the life I tell you of passed by,
Unstained by sordid strife or misery;
Sad, because though a glorious end it tells,
Yet on the end of glorious life it dwells,
And striving through all things to reach the best
Upon no midway happiness will rest.'

WILLIAM JULIUS MICKLE
[1735–1788]

from *Cumnor Hall,*
quoted in 'Introduction to Kenilworth' by Sir Walter Scott

The dews of summer night did fall;
  The moon, sweet regent of the sky,
Silver'd the walls of Cumnor Hall,
  And many an oak that grew thereby.

Now nought was heard beneath the skies,
  The sounds of busy life were still,
Save an unhappy lady's sighs,
  That issued from that lonely pile.

'Leicester,' she cried, 'is this thy love
  That thou so oft has sworn to me,
To leave me in this lonely grove,
  Immured in shameful privity?

'No more thou com'st with lover's speed,
  Thy once beloved bride to see;
But be she alive, or be she dead,
  I fear, stern Earl, 's the same to thee.

'At court, I'm told, is beauty's throne,
  Where every lady's passing rare,
That Eastern flowers, that shame the sun,
  Are not so glowing, not so fair.

'Then, Earl, why didst thou leave the beds
  Where roses and where lilies vie,
To seek a primrose, whose pale shades
  Must sicken when those gauds are by?

''Mong rural beauties I was one,
  Among the fields wild flowers are fair;
Some country swain might me have won,
  And thought my beauty passing rare.

'But, Leicester, (or I much am wrong,)
    Or 'tis not beauty lures thy vows;
Rather ambition's gilded crown
    Makes thee forget thy humble spouse.

'My spirits flag – my hopes decay –
    Still that dread death-bell smites my ear
And many a boding seems to say,
    "Countess, prepare, thy end is near!" '

Thus sore and sad that lady grieved,
    In Cumnor Hall, so lone and drear;
And many a heartfelt sigh she heaved,
    And let fall many a bitter tear.

And ere the dawn of day appear'd
    In Cumnor Hall, so lone and drear,
Full many a piercing scream was heard,
    And many a cry of mortal fear.

The death-bell thrice was heard to ring,
    An aerial voice was heard to call,
And thrice the raven flapp'd its wing
    Around the towers of Cumnor Hall.

The mastiff howl'd at village door,
    The oaks were shatter'd on the green;
Woe was the hour – for never more
    That hapless Countess e'er was seen!

And in that Manor now no more
    Is cheerful feast and sprightly ball;
For ever since that dreary hour
    Have spirits haunted Cumnor Hall.

The village maids, with fearful glance,
   Avoid the ancient moss-grown wall;
Nor ever lead the merry dance
   Among the groves of Cumnor Hall.

Full many a traveller oft hath sigh'd,
   And pensive wept the Countess' fall,
As wand'ring onwards they've espied
   The haunted towers of Cumnor Hall.

GEORGE WITHER
[1588–1667]

from *The Occasion of This Work*

I was so happy to that Ford I came,
Which of the labouring Ox doth bear the name.
It is a spring of knowledge that imparts
A thousand several sciences and arts,
A pure, clear fount, whose water is by odds
Far sweeter than the nectar of the gods;
Or rather (truly to entitle it)
It is the wholesome nursery of wit.

    There once arriv'd, in years and knowledge raw,
I fell to wond'ring at each thing I saw;
And for my learning made a month's vacation,
In noting of the placc's situation,
The palaces and temples that were due
Unto the wise Minerva's hallow'd crew,
Their cloisters, walks and groves; all which survey'd,
And in my new admittance well a-paid;
I did (as other idle freshmen do)
Long to go see the bell of Osney too;
And yet for certainty I cannot tell
That e'er I drank at Aristotle's well;
And that perhaps may be the reason why
I know so little in philosophy.
Yet old Sir Harry Bath was not forgot,
In the remembrance of whose wond'rous shot,
The forest by (believe it they that will)
Was nam'd Shot-over, as we call it still.

But having this experience, and withall
Atchiev'd some cunning at the tennis-ball,
My tutor (telling me I was not sent
To have my time there vain and idly spent)
From childish humours gently call'd me in,
And with his brave instructions did begin
To teach, and by his good persuasion sought
To bring me to a love of what he taught.

SIR ARTHUR QUILLER-COUCH
[1863–1944]

'Behold! I am not one that goes to Lectures'

Behold! I am not one that goes to Lectures or the
    pow-wow of Professors.
  The elementary laws never apologize: neither do
    I apologize.
I find letters from the Dean dropt on my table – and
    every one is signed by the Dean's name –
  And I leave them where they are; for I know that
    as long as I stay up
    Others will punctually come for ever and ever.
      I am one who goes to the river,
      I sit in the boat and think of 'life' and of
      'time.'
  How life is much, but time is more; and the begin-
    ning is everything,
    But the end is something.
I loll in the Parks, I go to the wicket, I swipe.
I see twenty-two young men from Foster's watching
    me, and the trousers of the twenty-two
    young men,
I see the Balliol men *en masse* watching me. – The
    Hottentot that loves his mother, the un-
    tutored Bedowee, the Cave-man that
    wears only his certificate of baptism, and
    the shaggy Sioux that hangs his testamur
    with his scalps.
I see the Don who ploughed me in Rudiments watch-
    ing me: and the wife of the Don who
    ploughed me in Rudiments watching me.
I see the rapport of the wicket-keeper and umpire.
  I cannot see that I am out.
Oh! you Umpires!
I am not one who greatly cares for experience, soap,
    bull-dogs, cautions, majorities, or a gradu-
    ated Income Tax.

The certainty of space, punctuation, sexes, institutions,
    copiousness, degrees, committees, delica-
    tesse, or the fetters of rhyme –
For none of these do I care: but least for the fetters
    of rhyme.
    Myself only I sing. Me Imperturbe! Me
    Prononcé!
    Me progressive and the depth of me progressive,
    And the βάθος, *Anglicé* bathos
    Of me hirsute, nakedly whooping,
Me over the tiles to the Cosmos endlessly whooping
    The song of Simple Enumeration.

WYSTAN HUGH AUDEN
[1907–1973]

Poem (for Benjamin Britten)

Underneath the abject willow,
　Lover, sulk no more;
Act from thought should quickly follow:
　What is thinking for?
Your unique and moping station
　Proves you cold;
　Stand up and fold
Your map of desolation.

Bells that toll across the meadows
　From the sombre spire,
Toll for those unloving shadows
　Love does not require.
All that lives may love; why longer
　Bow to loss
　With arms across?
Strike and you shall conquer.

Geese in flocks above you flying
　Their direction know;
Brooks beneath the thin ice flowing
　To their oceans go;
Coldest love will warm to action,
　Walk then, come,
　No longer numb,
Into your satisfaction.

GERARD MANLEY HOPKINS
[1844–1889]

To Oxford

(i)
New-dated from terms that reappear,
More sweet-familiar grows my love to thee,
And still thou bind'st me to fresh fealty
With long-superfluous ties, for nothing here
Nor elsewhere can thy sweetness unendear.
This is my park, my pleasaunce; this to me
As public is my greater privacy,
All mine, yet common to my every peer.
Those charms accepted of my inmost thought,
The towers musical, quiet-walled grove,
The window-circles, these may all be sought
By other eyes, and other suitors move,
And all like me may boast, impeached not,
Their special-general title to thy love.

(ii)
Thus, I come underneath this chapel-side,
So that the mason's levels, courses, all
The vigorous horizontals, each way fall
In bows above my head, as falsified
By visual compulsion, till I hide
The steep-up roof at last behind the small
Eclipsing parapet; yet above the wall
The sumptuous ridge-crest leave to poise and ride.
None besides me this bye-ways beauty try.
Or if they try it, I am happier then:
The shapen flags and drillèd holes of sky,
Just seen, may be to many unknown men
The one peculiar of their pleasured eye,
And I have only set the same to pen.

THOMAS HERBERT WARREN
[1853–1930]

May-Day on Magdalen Tower
Written for Mr Holman Hunt's Picture

Morn of the year, of day and May the prime!
   How fitly do we scale the steep dark stair!
   Into the brightness of the matin air,
To praise with chanted hymn and echoing chime,
Dear Lord of Light, Thy lowlihead sublime
   That stoop'd erewhile our life's frail weed to wear!
   Sun, cloud, and hill, all things Thou framest so fair,
With us are glad and gay, greeting the time.

The college of the lily leaves her sleep;
   The grey tower rocks and trembles into sound,
   Dawn-smitten Memnon of a happier hour;
Through faint-hued fields the silver waters creep;
   Day grows, birds pipe, and robed anew and crown'd,
   Green Spring trips forth to set the world aflower.

Oxford High Street

ROBERT SOUTHEY
[1774–1843]

For a Monument at Oxford

Here Latimer and Ridley in the flames
Bore witness to the truth. If thou hast walk'd
Uprightly through the world, proud thoughts of joy
Will fill thy breast in contemplating here
Congenial virtue. But if thou hast swerved
From the right path, if thou hast sold thy soul,
And served, with hireling and apostate zeal,
The cause thy heart disowns, – oh! cherish well
The honourable shame that sure this place
Will wake within thee, timely penitent,
And let the future expiate the past.

JOHN CROWE RANSOM
[1888–1976]

Philomela

Procne, Philomela, and Itylus,
Your names are liquid, your improbable tale
Is recited in the classic numbers of the nightingale.
Ah, but our numbers are not felicitous,
It goes not liquidly for us.

Perched on a Roman ilex, and duly apostrophized,
The nightingale descanted unto Ovid;
She has even appeared to the Teutons, the swilled and gravid;
At Fontainebleau it may be the bird was gallicized;
Never was she baptized.

To England came Philomela with her pain,
Fleeing the hawk her husband; querulous ghost,
She wanders when he sits heavy on his roost,
Utters herself in the original again,
The untranslatable refrain.

Not to these shores she came! this other Thrace,
Environ barbarous to the royal Attic;
How could her delicate dirge run democratic,
Delivered in a cloudless boundless public place
To an inordinate race?

I pernoctated with the Oxford students once,
And in the quadrangles, in the cloisters, on the Cher,
Precociously knocked at antique doors ajar,
Fatuously touched the hems of the hierophants,
Sick of my dissonance.

I went out to Bagley Wood, I climbed the hill;
Even the moon had slanted off in a twinkling,
I heard the sepulchral owl and a few bells tinkling,
There was no more villainous day to unfulfil,
The diuturnity was still.

Up from the darkest wood where Philomela sat,
Her fairy numbers issued. What then ailed me?
My ears are called capacious but they failed me,
Her classics registered a little flat!
I rose, and venomously spat.

Philomela, Philomela, lover of song,
I am in despair if we may make us worthy,
A bantering breed sophistical and swarthy;
Unto more beautiful, persistently more young,
Thy fabulous provinces belong.

JOHN BETJEMAN
[b. 1906]

May-Day Song for North Oxford
(Annie Laurie Tune)

Belbroughton Road is bonny, and pinkly bursts the spray
Of prunus and forsythia across the public way,
For a full spring-tide of blossom seethed and departed hence,
Leaving land-locked pools of jonquils by sunny garden fence.

And a constant sound of flushing runneth from windows where
The toothbrush too is airing in this new North Oxford air
From Summerfields to Lynam's, the thirsty tarmac dries,
And a Cherwell mist dissolveth on elm-discovering skies.

Oh! well-bound Wells and Bridges! Oh! earnest ethical search
For the wide high-table λογος of St C. S. Lewis's Church.
This diamond-eyed Spring morning my soul soars up the slope
Of a right good rough-cast buttress on the housewall of my hope.

And open-necked and freckled, where once there grazed the cows,
Emancipated children swing on old apple boughs,
And pastel-shaded book rooms bring New Ideas to birth
As the whitening hawthorn only hears the heart beat of the earth.

E. J. SCOVELL
[b. 1907]

An Open-Air Performance of
'As You Like It'

Art is unmade
To nature and the wild again
On the scythed grass before
A lime and skeletal ash
And the wall, solid with flowering,
Of longer unmown grass
Fumy with parsley flowers,
A level light mist rising;
Where the young actors barefoot
Warm in their exaltation
Burn in the evening's chill.

The art the poet won
From wilderness dissolves again,
Unformed upon this formless stage
Confluent with all earth's air;
For infiltrating winds,
Laughter, mid-distant trains
Steal the speech from their voices
Being amateur, unsure,
And moths bemuse their faces,
And our attention loses
Stragglers to cloud and star.

Envoys of life
At their set hour the swifts fly over,
Possess the air above us
And fish-tailed, fast as sight,
Play in their foamy margins,
Their inter-tidal light;
While the flood-lamps yet hardly
Sophisticate earth's colours,
And we half ride with the birds

Over our audience faces,
Over the reckless words.

And when 'If you have been . . .'
Orlando cries, 'If ever been
Where bells have knolled to church . . .'
And sweet upon his words
The Christchurch evening bell
Answers the homesick youth
Like rhyme confirming verse,
Evidence crowning truth,
It seems to our delight
As though the poet's earth
And ours lay in one night;

As though we had heard
The bell before the words were made
With him. Therefore I love
All loose ends, distractions
At such performances,
All their imperfections;
And if we bring our children,
Their soft and stubborn questions
Threading the marble words;
And art delivered up
To nature and the wild again.

ALEXANDER POPE
[1688–1744]

Upon the Duke of Marlborough's House at Woodstock

Atria longè patent; sed nec cœnantibus usquam
Nec somno locus est: quàm bene non habitas!

MART. *Epig.*

See, sir, here's the grand approach,
This way is for his Grace's coach;
There lies the bridge, and here's the clock,
Observe the lion and the cock,
The spacious court, the colonnade,
And mark how wide the hall is made!
The chimneys are so well designed,
They never smoke in any wind.
This gallery's contrived for walking,
The windows to retire and talk in;
The council-chamber for debate,
And all the rest are rooms of state.

'Thanks, sir,' cried I, ''tis very fine,
But where d'ye sleep, or where d'ye dine?
I find by all you have been telling,
That 'tis a house, but not a dwelling.'

RONALD ARBUTHNOTT KNOX
[1888–1957]

Limerick on Idealism

There was once a man who said 'God
Must think it exceedingly odd
   If he finds that this tree
   Continues to be
When there's no one about in the Quad.'

The Answer:

Dear Sir, Your astonishment's odd:
I am always about in the Quad.
   And that's why the tree
   Will continue to be,
Since observed by Yours faithfully, God.

Anon (from *Oxford Dictionary of Quotations*)

WYSTAN HUGH AUDEN
[1907–1973]

Oxford

Nature is so near: the rooks in the college garden
Like agile babies still speak the language of feeling;
By the tower the river still runs to the sea and will run,
   And the stones in that tower are utterly
   Satisfied still with their weight.

And the minerals and creatures, so deeply in love with their lives
Their sin of accidie excludes all others,
Challenge the nervous students with a careless beauty,
   Setting a single error
   Against their countless faults.

O in these quadrangles where Wisdom honours herself
Does the original stone merely echo that praise
Shallowly, or utter a bland hymn of comfort,
   The founder's equivocal blessing
   On all who worship Success?

Promising to the sharp sword all the glittering prizes,
The cars, the hotels, the service, the boisterous bed,
Then power to silence outrage with a testament,
   The widow's tears forgotten,
   The fatherless unheard.

Whispering to chauffeurs and little girls, to tourists and dons,
That Knowledge is conceived in the hot womb of Violence
Who in a late hour of apprehension and exhaustion
   Strains to her weeping breast
   The blue-eyed darling head.

And is that child happy with his box of lucky books
And all the jokes of learning? Birds cannot grieve:
Wisdom is a beautiful bird; but to the wise
      Often, often is it denied
      To be beautiful or good.

Without are the shops, the works, the whole green county
Where a cigarette comforts the guilty and a kiss the weak;
There thousands fidget and poke and spend their money:
      Eros Paidagogos
      Weeps on his virginal bed.

Ah, if that thoughtless almost natural world
Would snatch his sorrow to her loving sensual heart!
But he is Eros and must hate what most he loves;
      And she is of Nature; Nature
      Can only love herself.

And over the talkative city like any other
Weep the non-attached angels. Here too the knowledge of death
Is a consuming love: And the natural heart refuses
      The low unflattering voice
      That rests not till it find a hearing.

ROBERT BRIDGES
[1844–1930]

A Water-Party

Let us, as by this verdant bank we float,
Search down the marge to find some shady pool
Where we may rest awhile and moor our boat,
And bathe our tired limbs in the waters cool.
      Beneath the noonday sun,
      Swiftly, O river, run!

Here is a mirror for Narcissus, see!
I cannot sound it, plumbing with my oar.
Lay the stern in beneath this bowering tree!
Now, stepping on this stump, we are ashore.
      Guard, Hamadryades,
      Our clothes laid by your trees!

How the birds warble in the woods! I pick
The waxen lilies, diving to the root.
But swim not far in the stream, the weeds grow thick,
And hot on the bare head the sunbeams shoot.
      Until our sport be done,
      O merry birds, sing on!

If but to-night the sky be clear, the moon
Will serve us well, for she is near the full.
We shall row safely home; only too soon, –
So pleasant 'tis, whether we float or pull.
      To guide us through the night,
      O summer moon, shine bright!

LAURENCE BINYON
[1869–1943]

Bab-Lock-Hythe

In the time of wild roses
As up Thames we travelled
Where 'mid water-weeds ravelled
The lily uncloses,

To his old shores the river
A new song was singing,
And young shoots were springing
On old roots for ever.

Dog-daisies were dancing,
And flags flamed in cluster,
On the dark stream a lustre
Now blurred and now glancing.

A tall reed down-weighing,
The sedge-warbler fluttered;
One sweet note he uttered,
Then left it soft-swaying.

By the bank's sandy hollow
My dipt oars went bleating,
And past our bows fleeting
Blue-backed shone the swallow.

High woods, heron-haunted,
Rose, changed, as we rounded
Old hills greenly mounded,
To meadows enchanted;

A dream ever moulded
Afresh for our wonder,
Still opening asunder
For the stream many-folded;

Till sunset was rimming
The West with pale flushes;
Behind the black rushes
The last light was dimming;

And the lonely stream, hiding
Shy birds, grew more lonely,
And with us was only
The noise of our gliding.

In cloud of gray weather
The evening o'erdarkened.
In the stillness we hearkened;
Our hearts sang together.

MATTHEW ARNOLD
[1822–1888]

from *Thyrsis*

A Monody, *to commemorate the author's friend,*
Arthur Hugh Clough, *who died at Florence,* 1861

How changed is here each spot man makes or fills!
  In the two Hinkseys nothing keeps the same;
    The village street its haunted mansion lacks,
  And from the sign is gone Sibylla's name,
    And from the roofs the twisted chimney-stacks –
      Are ye too changed, ye hills?
  See, 'tis no foot of unfamiliar men
    To-night from Oxford up your pathway strays!
    Here came I often, often, in old days –
Thyrsis and I; we still had Thyrsis then.

Runs it not here, the track by Childsworth Farm,
  Past the high wood, to where the elm-tree crowns
    The hill behind whose ridge the sunset flames?
  The signal-elm, that looks on Ilsley Downs,
    The Vale, the three lone weirs, the youthful Thames? –
      This winter-eve is warm,
  Humid the air! leafless, yet soft as spring,
  The tender purple spray on copse and briers!
    And that sweet city with her dreaming spires,
She needs not June for beauty's heightening,

Lovely all times she lies, lovely to-night! –
  Only, methinks, some loss of habit's power
    Befalls me wandering through this upland dim.
  Once pass'd I blindfold here, at any hour;
    Now seldom come I, since I came with him.
      That single elm-tree bright
  Against the west – I miss it! is it gone?

We prized it dearly; while it stood, we said,
    Our friend, the Gipsy-Scholar, was not dead;
While the tree lived, he in these fields lived on.

Too rare, too rare, grow now my visits here,
    But once I knew each field, each flower, each stick;
        And with the country-folk acquaintance made
By barn in threshing-time, by new-built rick.
        Here, too, our shepherd-pipes we first assay'd.
            Ah me! this many a year
My pipe is lost, my shepherd's holiday!
        Needs must I lose them, needs with heavy heart
        Into the world and wave of men depart;
But Thyrsis of his own will went away.

        *   *   *

. . . I know the wood which hides the daffodil,
        I know the Fyfield tree,
I know what white, what purple fritillaries
    The grassy harvest of the river-fields,
        Above by Ensham, down by Sandford, yields,
And what sedged brooks are Thames's tributaries;

I know these slopes; who knows them if not I? –
    But many a dingle on the loved hill-side,
        With thorns once studded, old, white-blossom'd trees,
Where thick the cowslips grew, and far descried
        High tower'd the spikes of purple orchises,
            Hath since our day put by
The coronals of that forgotten time;
        Down each green bank hath gone the ploughboy's team,
        And only in the hidden brookside gleam
Primroses, orphans of the flowery prime.

Where is the girl, who by the boatman's door,
    Above the locks, above the boating throng,
        Unmoor'd our skiff when through the Wytham flats,

Red loosestrife and blond meadow-sweet among
   And darting swallows and light water-gnats,
      We track'd the shy Thames shore?
Where are the mowers, who, as the tiny swell
   Of our boat passing heaved the river-grass,
      Stood with suspended scythe to see us pass? –
They all are gone, and thou art gone as well!

Yes, thou art gone! and round me too the night
   In ever-nearing circle weaves her shade.
      I see her veil draw soft across the day,
   I feel her slowly chilling breath invade
      The cheek grown thin, the brown hair sprent with grey;
        I feel her finger light
Laid pausefully upon life's headlong train; –
      The foot less prompt to meet the morning dew,
      The heart less bounding at emotion new,
And hope, once crush'd, less quick to spring again.

And long the way appears, which seem'd so short
   To the less practised eye of sanguine youth;
      And high the mountain-tops, in cloudy air,
The mountain-tops where is the throne of Truth,
      Tops in life's morning-sun so bright and bare!
        Unbreachable the fort
Of the long-batter'd world uplifts its wall;
      And strange and vain the earthly turmoil grows,
      And near and real the charm of thy repose,
And night as welcome as a friend would fall.

          *   *   *

Too rare, too rare, grow now my visits here!
   'Mid city-noise, not, as with thee of yore,
      Thyrsis! in reach of sheep-bells is my home.
   – Then through the great town's harsh, heart-wearying roar,
      Let in thy voice a whisper often come,
        To chase fatigue and fear:

Why faintest thou? I wander'd till I died.
  Roam on! The light we sought is shining still.
    Dost thou ask proof? Our tree yet crowns the hill,
Our Scholar travels yet the loved hill-side.

ANNE RIDLER
[b. 1912]

Bathing in the Windrush

Their lifted arms disturb the pearl
And hazel stream
And move like swanbeams through the yielding
Pool above the water's whirl
As water swirls and falls through the torn field.

Earth bears its bodies as a burden:
Arms on a bright
Surface are from their shadows parted,
Not as the stream transforms these children
But as time divides the echo from the start.

Smiling above the water's brim
The daylight creatures
Trail their moonshine limbs below;
That melt and waver as they swim
And yet are treasures more possessed than shadows.

This wonder is only submarine:
Drawn to the light
Marble is stone and moons are eyes.
These are like symbols, where half-seen
The meaning swims, and drawn to the surface, dies.

DAVID GASCOYNE
[b. 1916]

Oxford: A Spring Day
For Bill

The air shines with a mild magnificence . . .
Leaves, voices, glitterings . . . And there is also water
Winding in easy ways among much green expanse,

Or lying flat, in small floods, on the grass;
Water which in its widespread crystal holds the whole soft song
Of this swift tremulous instant of rebirth and peace.

Tremulous – yet beneath, how deep its root!
Timelessness of an afternoon! Air's gems, the walls' bland grey,
Slim spires, hope-coloured fields: these belong to no date.

THOMAS TICKELL
[1686–1740]

from *Oxford*

Aloft in state the airy towers arise,
And with new lustre deck the wondering skies.
Lo, to what height the schools ascending reach!
Built with that art which they alone can teach;
The lofty dome expands her spacious gate
Where all the decent Graces jointly wait;
In every shape the god of Art resorts,
And crowds of sages till the extended courts.
   With wonders fraught the bright Museum see,
Itself the greatest curiosity,
Where Nature's choicest treasures all combin'd
Delight, at once, and quite confound the mind;
Ten thousand splendors strike the dazzled eye,
And form on earth another Galaxy.
   Here colleges in sweet confusion rise,
There temples seem to reach their native skies;
Spires, towers, and groves compose the various shew,
And mingled prospects charm the doubting view.
Who can deny their characters divine,
Without resplendent, and inspir'd within?
But since above my weak and artless lays,
Let their own poets sing their equal praise.

THOMAS LOVE PEACOCK
[1785–1866]

from *The Genius of the Thames*

Flow proudly, Thames! the emblem bright
   And witness of succeeding years!
Flow on, in freedom's sacred light,
   Nor stained with blood, nor swelled with tears.
Sweet is thy course, and clear, and still,
By Ewan's old neglected mill:
Green shores thy narrow stream confine,
Where blooms the modest eglantine,
And hawthorn-boughs o'ershadowing spread,
To canopy thy infant bed.
Now peaceful hamlets wandering through,
And fields in beauty ever new,
Where Lechlade sees thy current strong
First waft the unlabouring bark along;
Thy copious waters hold their way
Tow'rds Radcote's arches, old and grey,
Where triumphed erst the rebel host,
When hapless Richard's hopes were lost,
And Oxford sought, with humbled pride,
Existence from thy guardian tide.

JOHN WAIN
[b. 1925]

Nuffield
(from a group of poems about Oxford)

Before he came, the country and the town
Had settled down to something like accord.
A river slow but deep enough to drown:
Roads, markets. Barns where harvest could be stored.

November coal-smoke, river-mist in June
Made one flat sea beneath the pigeon's flight.
Steeple and anvil rang to the one tune.
St Aldate's heard the foxes bark at night.

Against this treaty Nuffield launched his war:
His weapons progress, profits, trusts and banks:
His prizes sales, promotions, more, more, more:
The cars rolled through the streets like tinny tanks.

What did their Leader dream of? With what shapes
People the empty spaces of the sky?
Nymph radiator-caps? Satiric apes?
What made him laugh? And did he ever cry?

If so, at what? At losses, or at fears?
What would the sadness be, of such a mind?
Petrol and money dripped away his years:
What knowledge could he lose, what secret find?

He died. We live among the things he willed.
Concrete and tyres. Shrouded in pastoral names
(Rose Hill and Blackbird Leys) the world he killed
Mocks us. *Sick hurry and divided aims.*

SAMUEL JOHNSON
[1709–1784]

from *The Vanity of Human Wishes*

When first the college rolls receive his name,
The young enthusiast quits his ease for fame;
Through all his veins the fever of renown
Burns from the strong contagion of the gown;
O'er Bodley's dome his future labours spread,
And Bacon's mansion trembles o'er his head.
Are these thy views? proceed, illustrious youth,
And virtue guard thee to the throne of Truth!
Yet should thy soul indulge the gen'rous heat,
Till captive Science yields her last retreat;
Should Reason guide thee with her brightest ray,
And pour on misty Doubt resistless day;
Should no false Kindness lure to loose delight,
Nor Praise relax, nor Difficulty fright;
Should tempting Novelty thy cell refrain,
And Sloth effuse her opiate fumes in vain;
Should Beauty blunt on fops her fatal dart,
Nor claim the triumph of a letter'd heart;
Should no Disease thy torpid veins invade,
Nor Melancholy's phantoms haunt thy shade;
Yet hope not life from grief or danger free,
Nor think the doom of man revers'd for thee:
Deign on the passing world to turn thine eyes,
And pause awhile from letters, to be wise;
There mark what ills the scholar's life assail,
Toil, envy, want, the patron, and the jail.
See nations slowly wise, and meanly just,
To buried merit raise the tardy bust.
If dreams yet flatter, once again attend,
Hear Lydiat's life, and Galileo's end.

An Oxford undergraduate

SALLY PURCELL
[b. 1944]

Oxford, Early Michaelmas Term

Impossible to register
each delicacy & shade,
each further richness of affectation
this feminine season adopts
for an audience captivated in advance
& hypnotised by hearsay, by skilful propaganda,
by its longing to play Hamlet
and be *really* melancholy.

Confident flirtations with a preciosity
already near to over-ripeness
increase the delight in imagined possession
of the inherited magic world;
whose soul and typewriter will vibrate first
to appraise in College garden
some sere and yellow leaf,
as the aesthetes flower gently?

ARTHUR HUGH CLOUGH
[1819–1861]

Commemoration Sonnets
Oxford, 1844

I

Amidst the fleeting many unforgot,
O Leonina! whether thou wert seen
Singling, upon the Isis' margent green,
From meaner flowers the frail forget-me-not,
Or, as the picture of a saintly queen,
Sitting, uplifting, betwixt fingers small,
A sceptre of the water-iris tall,
With pendent lily crowned of golden sheen;
So, or in gay and gorgeous gallery,
Where, amid splendours, like to those that far
Flame backward from the sun's invisible car,
Thou lookedst forth, as there the evening star;
Oh, Leonina! fair wert thou to see,
And unforgotten shall thine image be.

II

Thou whom thy danglers have ere this forgot,
O Leonina! whether thou wert seen
Waiting, upon the Isis' margent green,
The boats that should have passed there and did not;
Or at the ball, admiring crowds between,
To partner academical and slow
Teaching, upon the light Slavonic toe,
Polkas that were not, only should have been;
Or, in the crowded gallery crushed, didst hear
For bonnets white, blue, pink, the ladies' cheer
Multiplied while divided, and endure

(Thyself being seen) to see, not hear, rehearse
The long, long Proses, and the Latin Verse –
O Leonina! thou wert tired, I'm sure.

III

Not in thy robes of royal rich array,
As when thy state at Dresden thou art keeping;
Nor with the golden epaulettes outpeeping
From under pink and scarlet trappings gay
(Raiment of doctors) through the area led;
While galleries peal applause, and Phillimore
For the supreme superlative cons-o'er
The common-place-book of his classic head;
Uncrowned thou com'st, alone, or with a tribe
Of volant varlets scattering jest and jibe
Almost beside thee. Yet to thee, when rent
Was the Teutonic Caesar's robe, there went
One portion: and with Julius, thou to-day
Canst boast, I came, I saw, I went away!

WILFRED ROWLAND CHILDE
[b. 1890]

Vale
(for Eric Shepherd)

In Beckley from the high green woods
The eye looks down on sheeted floods,
Blue visionary solitudes,
Where many a thick-leaved hillock broods
On lonely Otmoor starkly grand,
And shining leagues of silent land,
Which the horizon's endless line
Does in an azure mist confine.

From Beckley the hid paths go down
To many a blessèd fairy town,
To many a hidden wandering way,
And the hushed flood of virgin Ray,
To Merton and to Ambrosden,
To Charlton, tower of fortunate men,
Lost in the gentian-coloured fen,
Whereof I am a citizen,
But shall not take youth there again.
(Rememberest thou, my soul, that noon
Watched by the still blue face of June,
The sacred water stealing slow,
The flowery dykes, how sweet they flow!
The starry lilies, golden and white,
The blossom of iris burning bright,
The dreaming distance infinite?)

From Beckley slowly wandering
Those roads meet many a pleasant thing,
Wood Eaton veiled in towering trees,
Noke nodding lapped in drowsy leas,
Cloaked Waterperry, nurse of peace,
And Elsfield, whence the traveller sees,

Faint, royal-crowned, majestical,
A distant vision, dear and small,
Apparent in the leafy dale,
Proud as a king's town in a tale,
The city of our blessedness,
The towers that are her gloriousness,
The spires that are her splendid joy –
So seems she to the gazing boy.

Ah, now my joy is not the same:
In Charlton under sunset-flame,
When all the dim marsh-lands aspire
Toward the orange western fire,
And in the vanèd tower the bell
Rings, and the hour is very well,
And the infinite plain is changèd all
To a vast blue blossom magical,
And a few stars shine, and the spring-dews fall:
In Beckley, when the flowers are out,
And in rich woods the cuckoos shout,
And scattered all around appear
The dancing babes of the jubilant year,
Green spurges, hyacinths, orchises,
A glory in the shade of the trees:
Ah, now I cannot laugh and sing,
And drink the sweet earth triumphing:
For now I am a man and find
The world is not made after my mind,
As it is made after the mind of a boy.
Good-bye, my lovely sister joy!

Good-bye, good-bye, exalted hills,
Good-bye to that rare peace which fills
Young hearts rejoicing in lonely air.
O hills, I leave you something fair,
I leave you youth: many other boys

Come here with laughters, hopes and joys,
Fill the bare lands with happy noise,
Take here long rambling careless walks,
And tire their comrades with vast talks,
And drain the blue and dream the world,
And see great infinite hopes unfurled,
Drink beer and tea in lonely inns,
Dismiss the seven deadly sins,
Alter the universe at will,
(Geraniums on the window-sill,
In those wise taverns, O good-bye!)
May other folk be glad as I
For ever in those aëry lands,
While great Saint Mary glorious stands,
And doth victoriously complete
The splendour of the only street.
Vale to the blessed hills, then,
And Vale to the azure fen:
Vale is my only truth.
Good-bye, my lovely sister youth,
As kind to others may'st thou be,
As thou hast ever been to me!

WILLIAM BELL SCOTT
[1811–1890]

Woodstock Maze

'O never shall anyone find you then!'
　　Said he, merrily pinching her cheek;
'But why?' she asked, – he only laughed, –
　　'Why shall it be thus, now speak!'
'Because so like a bird art thou,
　　Thou must live within green trees,
With nightingales and thrushes and wrens,
　　And the humming of wild bees.'
　　　　Oh, the shower and the sunshine every day
　　　　Pass and pass, be ye sad, be ye gay.

'Nay, nay, you jest, no wren am I,
　　Nor thrush nor nightingale,
And rather would keep this arras and wall
　　'Tween me and the wind's assail.
I like to hear little Minnie's gay laugh,
　　And the whistle of Japes the page,
Or to watch old Madge when her spindle twirls,
　　And she tends it like a sage.'
　　　　Oh, the leaves, brown, yellow, and red, still fall,
　　　　Fall and fall over churchyard or hall.

'Yea, yea, but thou art the world's best Rose,
　　And about thee flowers I'll twine,
And wall thee round with holly and beech,
　　Sweet-briar and jessamine.'
'Nay, nay, sweet master, I'm no Rose,
　　But a woman indeed, indeed,
And love many things both great and small,
　　And of many things more take heed.'
　　　　Oh, the shower and the sunshine every day
　　　　Pass and pass, be ye sad, be ye gay.

Woodstock Maze

'Aye, sweetheart, sure thou sayest sooth,
 I think thou art even so!
But yet needs must I dibble the hedge,
 Close serried as hedge can grow.
Then Minnie and Japes and Madge shall be
 Thy merry-mates all day long,
And thou shalt hear my bugle-call
 For matin or even-song.'
  Oh, the leaves, brown, yellow, and red, still fall,
  Fall and fall over churchyard or hall.

Look yonder now, my blue-eyed bird,
 See'st thou aught by yon far stream?
There shalt thou find a more curious nest
 Than ever thou sawest in dream.'
She followed his finger, she looked in vain,
 She saw neither cottage nor hall,
But at his beck came a litter on wheels,
 Screened by a red silk caul;
He lifted her in by her lily-white hand,
 So left they the blythe sunny wall.
  Oh, the shower and the sunshine every day
  Pass and pass, be ye sad, be ye gay.

The gorse and ling are netted and strong,
 The conies leap everywhere,
The wild briar-roses by runnels grow thick;
 Seems never a pathway there.
Then come the dwarf oaks knotted and wrung
 Breeding apples and mistletoe,
And now tall elms from the wet mossed ground
 Straight up to the white clouds go.
  Oh, the leaves, brown, yellow, and red, still fall,
  Fall and fall over churchyard or hall.

'O weary hedge, O thorny hedge!'
  Quoth she in her lonesome bower,
'Round and round it is all the same;
  Days, weeks, have all one hour;
I hear the cushat far overhead,
  From the dark heart of that plane;
Sudden rushes of wings I hear,
  And silence as sudden again.
    Oh, the shower and the sunshine every day
    Pass and pass, be ye sad, be ye gay.

'Maiden Minnie she mopes by the fire,
  Even now in the warmth of June;
I like not Madge to look in my face,
  Japes now hath never a tune.
But, oh, he is so kingly strong,
  And, oh, he is kind and true;
Shall not my babe, if God cares for me,
  Be his pride and his joy too?
    Oh, the leaves, brown, yellow, and red, still fall,
    Fall and fall over churchyard or hall.

I lean my faint heart against this tree
  Whereon he hath carved my name,
I hold me up by this fair bent bough,
  For he held once by the same;
But everything here is dank and cold,
  The daisies have sickly eyes,
The clouds like ghosts down into my prison
  Look from the barred-out skies.
    Oh, the shower and the sunshine every day
    Pass and pass, be ye sad, be ye gay.

'I tune my lute and I straight forget
　　What I minded to play, woe's me!
Till it feebly moans to the sharp short gusts
　　Aye rushing from tree to tree.
Often that single redbreast comes
　　To the sill where my Jesu stands;
I speak to him as to a child; he flies,
　　Afraid of these poor thin hands!
　　　　Oh, the leaves, brown, yellow, and red, still fall,
　　　　Fall and fall over churchyard or hall.

'The golden evening burns right through
　　My dark chamber windows twain:
I listen, all round me is only a grave,
　　Yet listen I ever again.
Will he come? I pluck the flower-leaves off,
　　And at each, cry, yes, no, yes!
I blow the down from the dry hawkweed,
　　Once, twice, ah! it flyeth amiss!
　　　　Oh, the shower and the sunshine every day
　　　　Pass and pass, be ye sad, be ye gay.

'Hark! he comes! yet his footstep sounds
　　As it sounded never before!
Perhaps he thinks to steal on me,
　　But I'll hide behind the door.'
She ran, she stopped, stood still as stone –
　　It was Queen Eleänore;
And at once she felt that it was death
　　The hungering she-wolf bore!
　　　　Oh, the leaves, brown, yellow, and red, still fall,
　　　　Fall and fall over churchyard or hall.

RONALD ARBUTHNOTT KNOX
[1888–1957]

Megalomania
by a Fourth Year Man.
(after Milton)

Hence, vain Committee meetings,
Of politics and social fervour born,
Meals at the Grid, and grinds that break the morn:
Hence, peaceful punt and noisy Quad,
To some retreat by man untrod,
Some limbo yet impenetrate of Keating's.
But come, my goddess that shalt be,
Humaniores Literae;
Come, with lecture-haunting haste,
And note-books cunningly enlac'd,
Come with Hope and simple Faith
And philosophick Shibboleth,
And ancient History in thy train,
Pensive, sober, and humane.
When I rise, no punctual Dean
Shall summon me at 1.15,
No jealous pen the record keep
Betwixt my Matins and my sleep.
So to breakfast, and anon
I rise t' attend the drowsy don,
Telling his rosary evermore
Of Tacit, Grote, and Diodore:
Still will I walk, from dawn to dusk
In raiment sordid and subfusc,
Ever, in thought, the candid tie
Shall be my neck's phylactery.
And I will take, 'neath wintry skies,
My postmeridian exercise
To Ferry Hincksey, or the Parks,
Now in Oxon, now in Berks,
With an uncomplaining friend

Discoursing wisely of the End:
(Wherewith the nimble Stagirite
Commenc'd his work, and said, when night
O'ertook him prating of the Μέσον
'Let us begin' – the Second Lesson).
Then will I to my books again
Till the whisky'd hour of ten,
Or such time as the weary'd Progs
Call in their base-informing dogs.
Such life might well the Gods beseem.
Then to bed at night, to dream
Of Alphas struggling with a pair
Of Categories in the air,
Love-lorn Idealists, that seek
Presentations most unique,
And golfers playing, frantick souls,
Round Copulas of eighteen Wholes.
And ever, to delude my foes,
Wrap me in a cynick pose
Of intellectual despair,
Holier than hermit's shirt of hair.
These give me, and a score of dates,
And I will get a —— in Greats.

GRAHAM GREENE
[b. 1904]

Sonnet

All these belong to youth; all these I hate:
The constant dreams that change and interchange,
Taking the whole world in a little range,
Yet creeping up to bed when it grows late;
And short-lived loves that yet are over strong,
When all the mind is one old weary faction,
Fearful of peace, more fearful still of action,
Fighting beneath no banner, with no song.

But age is like a wreck within a bay;
The sails are down: they do not feel the wind;
There comes no whisper from a foolish Spain;
The wheel is broken: there's no course to lay;
Only the sunlight like a fish gold-finned
Gleams through the water, laughs, is gone again.

MAX BEERBOHM
[1872–1956]

To an Undergraduate Needing Rooms in Oxford
from 'Zuleika Dobson'
(A Sonnet in Oxfordshire Dialect)

Zeek w'ere thee will in t'Univūrsity,
Lad, thee'll not vind nôr bread nôr bed that matches
Them as thee'll vind, roight züre, at Mrs. Batch's . . .